Chinese Characters

METRO BOOKS
NEW YORK

Text: James Trapp
Project Editor: James Bennett
Design: Rajdip Sanghera

Metro Books
122 Fifth Avenue
New York, NY 10011

ISBN: 978-1-4351-1993-2

Printed and bound in China

10 9 8 7 6 5 4 3 2 1

TRADITIONAL CHINESE BOOKBINDING
This book has been produced using traditional Chinese bookbinding
techniques, using a method that was developed during the Ming
Dynasty (1368–1644) and remained in use until the adoption of
Western binding techniques in the early 1900s. In traditional Chinese
binding, single sheets of paper are printed on one side only, and each
sheet is folded in half, with the printed pages on the outside. The book
block is then sandwiched between two boards and sewn together
through punched holes close to the cut edges of the folded sheets.

Chinese Characters

THE ART AND MEANING OF HANZI

Introduction

New archaeological discoveries are changing our picture of China's history but, for the moment, it is universally accepted that the earliest form of Chinese characters are found on what are known as oracle bones from the Shang Dynasty (around 1500–1050 BCE). These are the shoulder blades of cattle and tortoise shells that were used for predicting the future. A heated metal point was applied to the surface of the bone or shell making it crack. From the way the cracks ran, priests would interpret the answers to questions, which could be as simple as, 'Will it rain tomorrow?' Some of the characters used on these bones are identical in form to those in use today: 王 *wáng*, meaning 'king', is a good example, and more than half of all modern characters are clearly related to them. Inscriptions cast into bronze vessels from the Western Zhou Dynasty (1066–771 BCE) are the next early form of character.

MÌNG (PRONOUNCED *MING*)
MEANING: LIFE, FATE

The many different states that grew up after the decline of the Western Zhou developed their own variations on the character systems. In 221 BCE, First Emperor Qin Shihuang unified China and, to help establish his control, declared a single universal form of character for all official purposes. From then on the development of the writing system can be traced as a fairly continuous process to the present day. The final major change came when the Communist Party of the People's Republic of China introduced a simplified character system. In order to increase literacy among the people, existing simplifications were adapted, standardized, and added to in two waves in the 1950s and 1960s. This resulted in the forms in use today throughout mainland China. Full-form traditional characters are still used in Taiwan, and by other Chinese communities outside the People's Republic. The characters in this book are written in the traditional full-form because, in general, they are more decorative and perhaps carry a little more of the mystery and tradition of the thousands of years of Chinese civilization they represent.

The basic structure of a Chinese character is in two parts, known as the radical and the phonetic. The phonetic is normally a pre-existing recognized character that is supposed to give an indication of how the character is pronounced. The radical indicates the basic concept behind the meaning of the character. In the traditional system there are 214 radicals. Some radicals have more than one form depending on where they occur in the character. For example, both 性 *xìng* and 志 *zhì* have the heart

HUĀ (PRONOUNCED *HW-AH*)
MEANING: FLOWER

radical on the left and at the bottom respectively. The "water" radical 水 *shuǐ* is more commonly seen as the three dots in 酒 *jiǔ* and the "fire" radical 火 *huǒ* often appears as four dots at the bottom as in 熱 *rè*. The phonetic only gives an approximate idea of how the character might be pronounced, and often is of no use at all. As an example of a character where the phonetic works, let's look at 銅 *tóng* meaning copper or bronze: 金 is the 'metal' radical and 同 is the phonetic, a character in its own right also pronounced *tóng* and meaning 'identical, the same'. But with the character 話, pronounced *huà* and meaning 'speech', 言 is the speech radical, but the phonetic 舌 by itself is pronounced *shé*.

XÌNG (PRONOUNCED *SING*)
MEANING: LUCKY

The sounds of the characters above are shown in the standard Romanization called pinyin. In the text of this book a pronunciation guide is given along with the pinyin because pinyin itself is not always pronounced as a Western reader might expect it to be. You will also have noticed the marks over the vowels in the examples given above. These indicate tone. Chinese is a tonal language, which means that changes in the tone and pitch with which you make a sound alter that sound's meaning. Mandarin Chinese has only four tones. To a Western ear, these are four different ways of saying the same sound; other dialects have more. The first tone, shown like this, *mā*, is a level tone as though holding a note when singing. The second tone, *má*, is

加油

JIĀ YÓU (PRONOUNCED *JAR YO*)
MEANING: COME ON!, GO!

a rising tone as though asking a question. The third tone, *mǎ*, drops and then rises, like a dip in a roller coaster. The fourth tone, *mà*, is a falling tone, as though you are annoyed or making an emphatic point. To the Chinese ear, these are not the same sound said four different ways, but four different sounds and represent completely different words. *Mā* (first tone) means mother; *má* (second tone) means hemp or numb; *mǎ* (third tone) means horse; *mà* (fourth tone) means to scold. Characters carry no indication of tone. In fact, you cannot tell at all from the sound of a word how it is written, nor from the form of its character how it is pronounced. The two have to be learned side by side through constant repetition and recognition.

In today's digital world Chinese characters may seem inconvenient and out of place, and it is pinyin that is used to type Chinese into computers and other modern communication devices. However the beauty, complexity, and 3,500-year tradition of 漢字 *hàn zì* are so much a part of China's cultural identity that it is unlikely they will ever truly be replaced.

WǓ (PRONOUNCED *WOO*)
MEANING: DANCE

Ài

ài (pronounced *aye*) meaning love

This is the universal character for love in all its aspects, physical, emotional, and idealistic. In various combinations it means to make love, lover or spouse, fan or enthusiast, or even patriot (someone who loves their country). Appropriately, in the very middle is the character for the heart. However, its radical, which is found at the top, is the claw or talon, suggesting, perhaps, a person in the fierce grip of emotion.

Bàng

bàng (pronounced *bung*) meaning brilliant,
great, excellent

This character illustrates the range of meanings a single
character can carry. Its original meaning is a stick or club,
and in more modern times a bat, such as a baseball or cricket
bat. It also means a cob of corn or an ear of maize.
However, in speech, its most common usage is as an all-
purpose expression of approval or admiration, meaning
great or excellent.

Biàn

biàn (pronounced *bee-en*) meaning change

This is the basic character for change of any kind and is found in compound words with meanings as varied as rebellion, chameleon, and transsexual. It is an old character and the idea of change embodied by 變 is an important idea in Confucius' concept of what embodies a proper man. In the Analects he writes: 'They must often change who would be constant in happiness or wisdom,' and 'Only the wisest and stupidest of men do not change.'

Bīng

bīng (pronounced *bing*) meaning ice

This is a very good example of a character that combines the meanings of its different parts to create a new word. Here, the two dots on the left-hand side, which are the 'freezing' radical, are combined with the character for water, resulting in a primary meaning of ice. In Chinese, ice carries the same connotations of purity as in English but not the suggestion of being emotionally uptight. So, in China it is a compliment to describe a woman as having 'flesh of ice and bones of jade.'

Bīng

bīng (pronounced *bing*) meaning soldier

As a language, Chinese works in concepts, so words get
their exact meaning from the way in which they are used
in a sentence. Here, although the translation of soldier has
been given, the character actually represents many different
aspects of warfare and the military. While this character
particularly refers to a private as opposed to an officer, it can
also mean army, weapons, military affairs, and even a pawn
on a chessboard.

Chán

chán (pronounced *charn*) meaning Zen

Although Zen is commonly believed to be a Japanese religion, it is originally Chinese. Zen is a form of Buddhism based on meditation, taught by the Indian monk Bodhidharma at the Shaolin Temple in northern China in the sixth century CE. There the shadow of Bodhidharma is said to be permanently imprinted on a wall because he sat so long in meditation. A 禪杖 *chán zhàng* is a stick used for waking someone up who has fallen asleep while meditating.

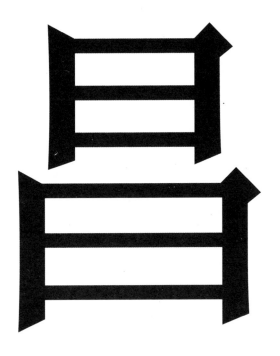

Chāng

chāng (pronounced *chaang*) meaning glorious,
prosperous

This character is not usually seen except in traditional
New Year greetings, though it was used regularly in the
years of Chairman Mao's leadership (1943–75) in slogans
praising the glory and prosperity of China under the 'Great
Helmsman.' It is, however, a very lucky character as well as a
pleasingly symmetrical one. Its meaning of glorious is clear
once you know that it is composed of two sun characters.

Chéng

chéng (pronounced *ch-ng*) meaning change, become

This is a very positive character, which complements 變 *biàn* in the compound word 變成 because it carries the meaning of bringing change to a successful completion. It implies permanence, or the accomplishment of something right and proper. It may also be more neutral but seldom carries negative connotations. 成年 *chéng nián* translates as 'complete years', which means to come of age, and an adult is a 成人 *chéng rén,* a finished person.

Dà

dà (pronounced *dah*) meaning great

This is a fundamental Chinese character that can be traced
back in recognizable form to the very earliest fully formed
character systems on oracle bones of the Shang Dynasty
(c. 1500–1066 BCE) and inscriptions cast into ritual bronze
vessels of the Western Zhou (1066–771 BCE). It is a pure
pictogram showing a man stretching his arms out to indicate
size (although we cannot be sure whether or not the original
man had just returned from an unsuccessful fishing trip).

Dào

dào (pronounced *dow*) meaning *dao* (*tao*) the way, reach, arrive

This is probably one of the most commonly recognized Chinese characters in the West, and also the most frequently mispronounced. 道 is a term used by both Daoism and Confucianism to represent the inexpressible yet inherently knowable true nature of the world. Knowledge of the Dao is achievable through 德 *dé*, virtue. The principal text of Daoism is Laozi's *Dao De Jing* – the classic of the Way and Virtue.

Fēng

fēng (pronounced *fung*) meaning wind

This elegant character seems to suit its meaning. It is a very versatile word, with a basic meaning of wind. It forms one half of feng shui, (literally wind and water), the ancient Chinese system of harmonizing the natural flow of energy. But it also means reputation, fame, taste, style, and gossip – all things that may symbolically be carried on the wind. If you want to wish someone 'Bon Voyage', 一帆風順 expresses hope that their sails will be filled by a good wind.

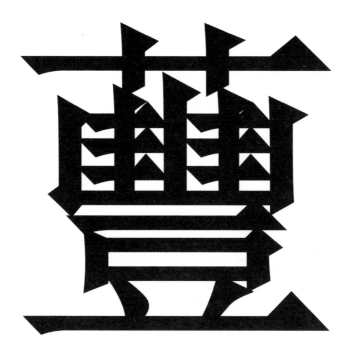

Fēng

fēng (pronounced *fung*) meaning abundant

This handsome and complex character is another of the auspicious symbols that appear frequently in New Year greetings and other sayings for good luck. Its original meaning of a crop or harvest can be discerned from its radical, which forms the bottom half, and is the character for peas, beans, and legumes. Its now more usual meaning of abundant, fruitful, or copious can be applied to anything from harvests and wealth to hair or a voluptuous figure.

Fèng

fèng (pronounced *fung*) meaning phoenix

The full name for the Chinese phoenix is 鳳凰 *fènghuáng*, the first character being the male bird and the second the female. The Chinese phoenix does not share the same mythology of rebirth through fire as the Western version, but it is the ruler of all the birds and ranks second only to the dragon among supernatural animals. The dragon came to represent the emperor and the phoenix the empress.

Fú

fú (pronounced *foo*) meaning good fortune

This character tops the list of characters to do with good fortune, both in phrases and standing by itself. Around New Year it can be seen on red posters pasted upside down on doorways. It is the only character that is still lucky when displayed this way because it creates a play on words. The phrase '*fú* turned upside down' sounds the same as the phrase '*fú* has arrived.' In another example of wordplay, which forms the basis of much traditional Chinese symbolism, flying bats (*fú*) denote good fortune.

Fù

fù (pronounced *foo*) meaning father

Hardly surprisingly, the character for father, along with that
for mother (see 母 *mù*) is another of the very earliest forms,
appearing regularly on oracle bones meaning both father
as a parent, and also as a respected older person or even an
ancestor. On one bone, the question posed is whether the
(presumably dissatisfied) spirit of Father Yi is responsible for
a toothache. The modern character derives from a pictogram
showing a hand holding a stick.

關係

Guān Xi

guān xi (pronounced *gwarn hsee*) meaning
connections

This two-character phrase means a kind of connection or
relationship, and it lies at the heart of Chinese society. It
is not used to describe relationships within the family, or
the normal give-and-take of social and professional status.
Instead it represents the informal and complex network
of friendships and obligations, outside your own personal
sphere of influence, through which things get done.

Guāng

guāng (pronounced *gwong*) meaning light,
radiance, glory

A simple yet powerful character, this is the basic word for
light or brightness. But it also covers symbolic brightness or
glory. This character has been used for centuries. In imperial
times it was used to mean the glory and enlightened rule of
the emperor. In modern scientific terms it occurs in phrases
such as 光電子 *guāng diàn zi* (photoelectrons) and 光盤
guāng pán (an optical disc or CD).

Hǎo

hǎo (pronounced *how*) meaning good

This is probably the first character and word that anyone studying Chinese learns. It is part of the basic Chinese greeting 你好 *nǐ hǎo*, literally 'you good,' meaning 'Hello.' Combining the two characters for woman on the left, and child on the right, this represents the mother-child relationship, which the Chinese consider to be the ultimate of all things. It is your all-purpose word in Chinese for expressing appreciation, approval, or agreement.

Hé

hé (pronounced *her*) meaning harmony

A very gentle character, this carries a very positive meaning covering aspects of harmony, peace, and gentleness, and things being as they should be all round. It has an underlying theme of connection and the order and unity of nature. At a much more everyday level it serves as the Chinese equivalent of 'and' and 'with'. This is another very good example of how the Chinese language functions through complex concepts rather than exact meanings.

Huā

huā (pronounced *hw-ah*) meaning flower

This character for flower or blossom is a good illustration of the standard formation of a Chinese character in radical and phonetic parts. The three strokes at the top are the grass radical, indicating a connection with plants and growing things, and the phonetic below is the character pronounced huà, meaning change. The popularity of flowers as decoration in art and design over the centuries has also given this character the meaning of pattern or ornamentation.

Huǒ

huǒ (pronounced *hw-or*) meaning fire

Fire is one of the Wǔ Xíng or Five Elements of Chinese philosophy and traditional medicine. The others are wood, earth, water, and metal. They are also used in martial arts, fengshui, astrology, and music, among other fields. Fire is connected with red, the direction of the south, and the planet Mars (whose name in Chinese is the Fire Planet). In traditional Chinese medicine, Fire is associated with youth and its dominant organs are the heart and the small intestine.

Jí

jí (pronounced *jee*) meaning auspicious

This simple and memorable character is another one of the most widely used lucky characters. It appears most frequently either on its own or in sayings used around Chinese New Year. A particularly useful all-purpose wish you might make for your family or friends is 万事大吉 *wàn shì dà jí* (literally, 10,000 things great lucky). In oracle bone form, according to one explanation, this character represents a weapon or weapons being stored away, symbolizing a time of peace.

Jí

jí (pronounced *jee*) meaning extreme, utmost

This indefinably pleasing character provides another excellent example of how meaning is dependent on context. It is most commonly used with the meaning of 'really' or 'extremely' – as in 好極了 *hǎo jíle* 'really good, great' or 餓極了 *è jíle* 'really hungry, starving'. But among other things, it is also the *jí* in 太極拳 *Taiji Quan*, the martial art and exercise form often called Tai Chi in the West, and also means the North or South Pole, the extreme points of the Earth.

Jiā

jiā (pronounced *jar*) meaning home, family

This character provides a lesson in social history. It is made up of two parts. The top three strokes represent a roof and the bottom half is the early character for a pig (imagine a sow lying down feeding her piglets). Together they have the meaning of house, home, and family. In ancient, and indeed not-so-ancient Chinese farming communities, the pig was the principal and most valuable source of meat and was kept not separately in a sty but in the farmhouse. Home is where the pig is!

加油

Jiā yóu

Jiā yóu (pronounced *jar yo*) meaning come on! go!

This is the all-purpose shout of encouragement or exhortation to speed – the equivalent of our 'Go!' and 'Step on it!' It can be used either just by itself or with the addition of the name of an individual, club or team. It literally means 'add oil', so before the invention of petrol and the car, it could be taken as adding oil to a fire to make it burn fiercer. However, since the Chinese for gas (petrol) is 汽油 *qì yóu* – 'vapour oil', stepping on the gas is the modern equivalent.

Jiàn

jiàn (pronounced *jen* like jenny) meaning sword

A classic radical-phonetic combination, the two strokes on the right of this character are the 'knife' radical, and the left side is formed by a character also pronounced *jian*. This is the character that one of the assassins is seen practicing writing in a sandbox at the beginning of the film 'Hero'. Bronze swords were one of the main weapons of early Chinese armies. Some of the swords dug up with the Terracotta Army were chrome-plated and still razor-sharp after 2200 years.

Jīn

jīn (pronounced *gin*) meaning gold, metal, money

This is another of the Five Elements. Metal is the element of old age, and its organs are the lungs and the large intestine. The primary emotions of Metal are grief or sadness and it has an association with decay. Venus is the metal planet. As well as having the general meaning of metal, 金 also specifically means gold and, by extension, money. The Chinese for the 2008 world financial crisis is 金融危機 *jīnróng wēijī,* which literally means 'the money mix danger situation.'

Jìng

jìng (pronounced *jing*) meaning respect

Respect is a vital part of the social and philosophical glue that has held Chinese society together, enabling it to survive as the longest continuous civilization in history. Respect in different forms underpins the teachings of Confucius: A ruler must respect his position and duties as ruler, and his subjects must respect him (義 *yì*); respect must be given to the correct observance of rites and ceremonies (禮 *lǐ*); and sons and daughters must show proper respect to their parents (孝 *xiào*).

Jiǔ

jiǔ (pronounced *joe*) meaning wine, alcohol

This character is normally translated as wine but refers to any kind of alcohol. Archaeology suggests that a fermented alcoholic drink made from millet was being produced in China 9,000 years ago, the earliest in any civilization. Wine played an important part in ancient rituals, and as early as 1600 BCE magnificent bronze vessels were produced for offerings of wine to ancestors. China still takes great pride in its distilled grain liquors, of which Maotai is the most famous. Many Westerners have been ambushed by their potency.

Kù

kù (pronounced *koo*) meaning cool!

Modern Chinese is not developing by adding new characters to its vocabulary but by adapting the meanings of existing characters. For example, 電 *diàn*, originally meaning lightning, became the general word for electricity. Here, because of it closeness in sound to the English, a character that originally meant cruel or tyrannical, and with an extended meaning of very or extreme, has in modern times taken on new life as an all-purpose expression of approval and agreement.

Lè/Yuè

lè/yuè (pronounced *ler/yweh*) meaning happy/music

Here is a single character with two very different pronunciations and two meanings that are distinct yet connected. *Le* can be read as meaning happy or happiness, but it is equally commonly used with the pronunciation *yue*, meaning music, its ancient meaning. Music and happiness are surely a natural pairing. Interestingly, with the addition of the 'grass' radical it means medicine, referring to the healing power of music in traditional Chinese medicine.

Léi

léi (pronounced *lay*) meaning thunder

This is a powerful-looking character that suits its meaning. Still in current use, it is an early pictogram showing falling rain over a field. The top half is the character for rain, which is also the common radical for most types of weather. The bottom half is the character for field and shows the division of a plot of land into four equal areas. Clearly the character's formation carries some ancient farmer's recognition of the significance of thunder.

Lěng

lěng (pronounced *lung*) meaning cold

Illustrating how radicals signify general meaning, this character has the same two-stroke 'ice' radical as 'bīng', ice. Here, however, the other half of the character is a phonetic component (*lǐng*), which, although close, shows the unreliability of this element in indicating how it should be pronounced. Cold is associated with the Yin aspect of Yin and Yang; keeping the correct balance of heat and cold is a fundamental principle of traditional Chinese medicine.

Lǐ

lǐ (pronounced *lee*) meaning rites, correct
behaviour

According to Confucius, 禮 *lǐ* – meaning rites and ritual, the
correct observance of them, and thus correct conduct in
general – was an essential requirement of a gentleman. He
said, 'Of the things brought about by the rites, harmony is
the most valuable.' The character came to mean ceremonies
of any kind and is now also used for presents given at
celebrations, such as birthdays and weddings.

Lì

lì (pronounced *lee*) meaning strength, power

One of the most basic of all Chinese characters, the simplicity of 力 *lì* contradicts its meaning. It is also one of the very earliest characters, appearing on oracle bones from the 2nd century BCE. It covers all kinds of strength, physical, mental, and spiritual, and also in modern usage roughly corresponds to the English word ending –ity, for example 能力 *nénglì* = to be able+strength = ability; 創造力 *chuàngzàolì* = create+strength = creativity.

Lóng

Lóng (pronounced *loong*) meaning dragon

Chinese dragons are different from Western dragons. They
do not have wings, they do not breathe fire, and they are not
evil. In fact, they are always associated with water. Though
fierce, they are seen as friendly guardian figures. One legend
tells that four great dragons became the four great rivers of
China in order to save the people during a drought. Dragons
were also the symbol of the emperors of China, and only an
imperial dragon is depicted with five claws on each foot.

Měi

měi (pronounced *may*) meaning beautiful, America

Probably best not to mention this when you are complimenting someone on their beauty, but the radical for this character is 羊, a sheep or goat, and the bottom half is 大, meaning big. One possible explanation for this strange construction is that in Chinese astrology, people born in the year of the goat have always been associated with good luck, grace, and beauty. The Chinese for America is 美國 *měiguó*, meaning beautiful country.

Míng

míng (pronounced *ming*) meaning bright

This elegant example is formed of two characters, 日 *rì*
the sun, and 月 *yuè* the moon. Together they mean bright,
brilliant, or clear. By extension, 明 *míng* also means to
understand. It is most familiar in the West as the name of the
Ming Dynasty (1368–1644 CE), one of the greatest periods of
Chinese civilization and the last native Chinese dynasty. Ming
porcelain is justifiably considered the greatest achievement
of the Chinese potter.

Mìng

mìng (pronounced *ming*) meaning life, fate

Another simple character loaded with powerful meaning, this covers all aspects of life in the sense of fate, divine will, or destiny. It is also the character for an official command or decree, presumably because these have the power to affect one's life or fate. According to a Daoist saying, 命不足道 *mìng bù zú dào,* 'one's fate in life is not more important than living correctly.'

Mǔ

mǔ (pronounced *moo*) meaning mother

Not surprisingly, this is another of the very earliest Chinese characters. In its oracle bone form it is a clear depiction of a kneeling woman. Even in its modern form, the two dots still represent the mother's nurturing breasts. It is also on oracle bones that one of China's most powerful female deities first appears: 西王母 *xī wáng mǔ*, the Queen Mother of the West. Once she was adopted by Daoism she gradually changed from being a fierce tiger-demon into a guardian of the Western Paradise and bringer of immortality and perfect peace.

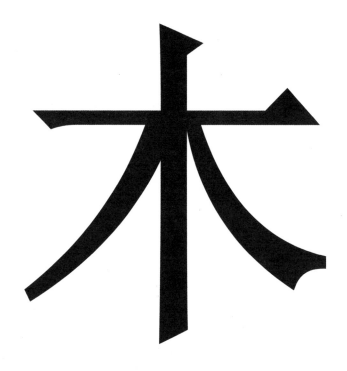

Mù

mù (pronounced *moo*) meaning wood

Wood is another of the Five Elements of Chinese philosophy and traditional medicine. It is associated with the liver and gall bladder, both of which the Chinese believe control our decision-making and planning for the future. Anger is the primary Wood emotion, its season is spring, and Jupiter is the Wood planet. For many centuries, wood was the building material of choice for even the grandest buildings in China.

Nán

nán (pronounced *naan*) meaning male

An ancient oracle bone pictogram, the character for man or male is composed of a field above the character for strength. The character therefore clearly illustrates the man's primary role in early agricultural society as the food provider. China prides itself on being the longest continuous civilization in history, and one curious example of this is that the character denoting 'man' from 1500 BCE is still the one used to indicate the men's room 3,500 years later.

Nǚ

nǚ (pronounced *nu* like queue)
meaning female, woman

As with the character for male (男 *nán*) this is a very early
pictogram, in this case depicting a seated female figure. The
earliest oracle bone form seems to show the figure bowing
with her hands crossed in front of her. This character forms
the male-female pair with 男, but a more direct parallel with
the male character is 妻 *qī* with the meaning of wife, which
originally depicted a woman holding a broom.

Píng ān

píng ān (pronounced *ping an*) meaning peace, harmony

Because there are so many homophones (words that sound the same but have different meanings) in Chinese, clarity is often achieved by using two- and three-character words. In these, each character retains its original meaning but combines to produce a more exact expression. Here 'even/flat' and 'peace' combine to give the phrase most commonly heard in the Chinese equivalent of 'Bon Voyage' 一路平安 *yí lù ping ān,* literally 'one road flat peace.'

Qì

qì (pronounced *chee*) meaning energy, Qi

This is probably one of the most widely recognized Chinese words thanks to the growing popularity of martial arts, feng shui and Traditional Chinese Medicine in the West. Literally, 氣 *qì* means steam, gas, or air, and the original pictogram shows the steam rising from rice as it cooks. It also refers to the fundamental energy or life force that the Chinese believe runs through everything. For example, control of the flow of 氣 *qì* through fixed energy channels, called meridians, is the basis of acupuncture.

Qián

qián (pronounced *chee-en*) meaning money

This character is now the general word for money. It originally meant specifically a copper cash, or coin. Before First Emperor Qin Shihuang united China in 221 BCE, different states used different shapes of coin, but he insisted only one currency could be used across his empire. The shape he decreed, a round coin with a square hole, remained the standard unit of currency for the next 2,250 years. Although the coin is no longer in use, it can still be seen in the logo of the Bank of China.

Qiáng

qiáng (pronounced *chee-ang*) meaning strong

The radical on the left-hand side of this character is 弓 *gōng* meaning bow, as in bow and arrow. The character's current meaning of strong reflects both the might of the bow as the principal attack weapon of early Chinese armies, and the strength required to use one. Reconstructions of Chinese crossbows of the third century BCE show that they had a range of more than 2,300ft (700m). This character also means mental and emotional strength.

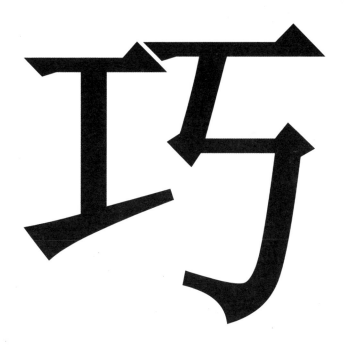

Qiǎo

qiǎo (pronounced *chee-ow*) meaning clever, skilled

This simple, oddly angular but pleasing character symbolizes both of the meanings of 'clever' in English: either ingenious and skilful, or cunning and devious. It is at the heart of many sayings and proverbs, such as 巧言不如直道 *qiǎo yán bù rú zhí dào,* 'clever words can't beat straight talking' and perhaps more controversially: 巧妻常伴拙夫眠 *qiǎo qī cháng bàn zhuō fū mián,* 'a clever wife often ends up with a stupid husband.'

Qīng

qīng (pronounced *ching*) meaning clear, pure

This character paints a picture of a beautiful clear stretch of water. The three dots on the left-hand side are the 'water' radical, and the right-hand phonetic component also seems to carry a similar meaning because, by itself, it is the symbol for that indefinable hue between blue and green. This character is also the name of the Qing Dynasty, which was established by the invading Manchus in 1644 and ended with the abdication of the last Emperor, Pu-Yi, in 1912.

Rè

rè (pronounced *rer*) meaning hot, heat

The four dots at the bottom of this character are one form of the 'fire' radical. Heat is an important concept in Traditional Chinese Medicine, and must be kept in balance. Not just the sun, but dryness, strong winds, and even extreme cold can all cause an excess of heat in the body which, the Chinese believe, will affect the heart, lungs and spleen. They believe that diet is particularly important in regulating heat, and chrysanthemum tea, green vegetables, apples, and bananas are all considered cooling foods.

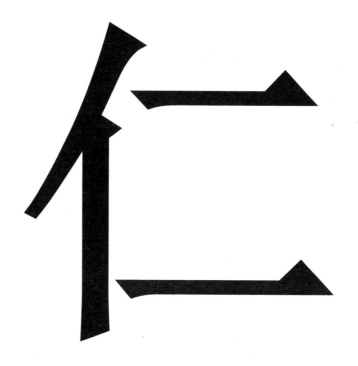

Rén

rén (pronounced *ren*) meaning benevolence

仁 *rén*, usually translated as benevolence or kindness, is one of the key virtues in Confucian thought. The construction of the character is highly significant: it is composed of the 'man' radical on the left, and the number two on the right. This is believed to indicate its meaning of the proper conduct and intentions between two people. Confucius believed that it was innate in humans and said: 'Rén is not far away; anyone who seeks it has already found it.' 仁 *rén* is the inward expression of Confucian ideals, while 禮 *lǐ* is the outward.

Rì

rì (pronounced *jrrr*) meaning sun, day

This character started as a pictogram showing the sun as a circle with a dot in the middle and four short rays. It quickly changed into this form, which is even found on oracle bones with the meaning of day. One inscription, entirely recognizably to modern Chinese readers, reads 今日其雨, meaning: 'Will it rain today?' The characters for Japan in both Chinese and Japanese are 日本, meaning 'sun root' or, more poetically, 'Land of the Rising Sun.'

Shí

shí (pronounced *shrr*) meaning stone, rock

This is another of those characters that looks exactly right for what it is supposed to mean, without any actual explanation why. The sound *shi* is the commonest in Mandarin Chinese. Even a fairly basic dictionary lists 58 different characters all pronounced *shi* in one of the four tones. There is a famous nonsense story consisting of 92 characters all pronounced *shi* which is intelligible only as characters – not when spoken – because unless you see the characters you cannot tell which meaning of *shi* is intended.

Shòu

shòu (pronounced *show*) meaning long life

This is probably the most popular of the lucky characters that appear on banners and posters during Chinese festivals and other auspicious occasions. It is also one of the most frequently used designs in jewels and painting, especially because there are many different stylized forms that can be used. A dictionary containing 10,001 different forms of the character from the Bronze Age (c. 2000–771 BCE) to the modern day was recently published in Beijing.

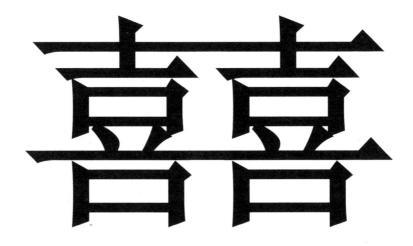

Shuāng Xǐ

shuāng xǐ (pronounced *sh-wong see*) meaning
double happiness

Strangely enough, one of the commonest good luck symbols
is a character that you cannot look up in a dictionary. It is
formed of two characters, 喜 *xǐ* 'happiness', written side by
side and sometimes joined together. It is known as 'double
happiness' and is, not surprisingly, the most important symbol
at weddings and anniversary celebrations. According to
tradition its origins go back to the Tang Dynasty (618–907 CE).

Shuǐ

shuǐ (pronounced *sh-way*) meaning water

This character was originally a pictogram in the form of three parallel wavy lines depicting flowing water. It is also one of the most common radicals in other characters, most often in its abbreviated form of three dots on the left-hand side. Water is another of the Five Elements, and its planet is Mercury. As you might expect, the Water organs are the kidneys and the bladder. Fear is the Water emotion and its season is winter. This element is also associated with death.

Sǐ

sǐ (pronounced *sssr*) meaning death

This character does not bode well. It suggests a burial in the way the character is formed, with the two lower parts looking as though they are below ground. In Chinese numerology, four is considered the most unlucky number because its pronunciation, *sì*, is only one tone away from 死 *sǐ*. Anything you buy in China that happens to display a number will be less expensive if it contains the number 4. In contrast, anything with the number 8, which is considered lucky, will be more expensive.

Tài

tài (pronounced *tie*) meaning supreme

This is the character 大 *dà*, meaning great, with an extra dash
for emphasis. 太陽 *tàiyáng* 'Supreme Yang' is the normal
word for the sun, while 太陰 *tàiyīn* 'Supreme Yin' is also used
for the moon, though less commonly. 太太 *tàitài* 'Supreme
Supreme' is the title for a married woman, the equivalent of
Mrs in English, and is also one of the words for wife.

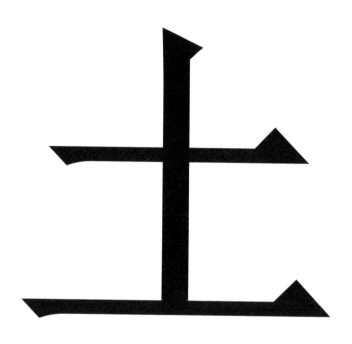

Tǔ

tǔ (pronounced *too*) meaning earth

Another of the Five Elements, Earth is associated with yellow,
and its planet is Saturn. In traditional Chinese medicine,
Earth is concerned with the spleen, pancreas, and stomach,
the organs of digestion. Its emotion is anxiety, and its stage
of life is adulthood. Unlike the other four elements, Earth is
not associated with a particular season, but with the period of
change between seasons every three months.

武術

Wǔ Shù

wǔ shù (pronounced *woo shoe*) meaning
martial arts

This is the general term for all the different forms of Chinese
combat, both armed and unarmed. Some forms can be
traced back to the very first dynasties of the Bronze Age
3,500 years ago. Perhaps the most famous in the West is what
we call Shaolin Kung Fu: 少林工夫. According to tradition,
monks of the Shaolin Temple near Zhengzhou in Henan
province first developed this form of martial art in the
seventh century CE.

Wǔ

wǔ (pronounced *woo*) meaning dance

This is an expressive character that seems to call to mind the formality of ritual dance. Formal and ritual dance played a very important role in court ceremonies starting in the Shang Dynasty (c. 1500–1066 BCE), while the wide range of different peoples living in China provided a huge variety of folk dances. Pottery tomb figures from the Tang Dynasty (618–907 CE) vividly conjure up the flamboyant and fantastic silk costumes of court dancers.

Xiào

xiào (pronounced *see-ow*) meaning smile, laugh

One explanation of the origin of this character is that the lower portion represents a man throwing his head back in laughter; the 'bamboo' radical of the upper portion is said to compare the swaying motion of bamboo with a person rocking with laughter. This character is often seen on posters and banners at festivals and ceremonies. There are many Chinese proverbs and sayings involving laughter, one intriguing example being: 'A woman who is always laughing is everybody's wife; a man who is always laughing is an idiot.'

Xiào

xiào (pronounced *see-ow*) meaning
filial piety, dutifulness

Doing one's duty is one of the most important concepts in
Confucianism, along with 仁 *rén*, 義 *yì*, and 禮 *lǐ*. Here, the
concept of filial piety, or duty to your parents or elders, is
indicated by the symbol for 'child' that forms the bottom
of the character. The *Xiao Jing*, or Classic of Filial Piety,
is one of the textbooks of Confucianism, possibly written
around 470 BCE.

Xîn

xîn (pronounced *sin*) meaning heart

One of the earliest and most primitive of characters, the original pictogram found on oracle bones is a very realistic drawing of a heart, which gradually evolved into this final form. In traditional Chinese medicine the heart is considered to be the organ of the emotions. The 'heart' radical, either in this form or in its even simpler form as a vertical line flanked by two dots, as in 性 *xìng*, is a reliable indicator that the character involves feelings and emotions.

Xīn

xīn (pronounced *sin*) meaning new

This is the first character in the Chinese phrase for Happy New Year, 新年快樂 *xīn nián kuài lè*, or New Year Happy, as it translates literally. It is another lucky character because optimism is everything at the New Year. For the same reason, it became a vastly overused word in China following the establishment of the People's Republic. Every initiative, great and small, began with this character in the hope that constant repetition would ensure that 'new' would also be understood as 'good' and 'successful'.

Xìn

xìn (pronounced *sin*) meaning belief, trust

This character clearly indicates that a man's word is his bond: the 'man' radical on the left qualifies the character for speech. More literally it also means a letter (the kind you send), this also being a person's words. In the former meaning it covers all kinds of belief, including philosophical and religious, and trust. In the latter, it has adapted with the changing times and is part of the word for an SMS text message: 短信 *duǎn xìn*, a short letter.

Xìng

xìng (pronounced *sing*) meaning sex

The way this character is put together, with the heart radical flanking the character for 'to be born,' displays the wide range of its meaning. 性 *xìng* represents humanity's inner nature, the correct cultivation of which is at the core of both Confucian and Daoist philosophy. The use of the same character to mean sex, both as gender and as sexual relations, acknowledges that sex is natural and free of guilt.

Xìng

xìng (pronounced *sing*) meaning lucky

A useful all-purpose lucky character, this also has the benefit of simplicity. It is also seen combined with the other popular 'good fortune' character 福 *fú* as 幸福, where a double helping of good luck leads to a meaning of happiness or well-being. By itself, 幸 *xìng* also has a generally optimistic meaning, as in 'hopefully, the tattooist will get this character right' in English, and the idea of fate smiling on one, as in 'luckily, the tattooist was Chinese.'

Xīng/Xìng

xīng/xìng (pronounced *sing*) meaning flourish, prosper

A solid and reassuring character, the tone with which it is read changes the meaning. Spoken using the first tone it means joyful, happy, or even passion, and in the fourth means flourish or prosper. Clearly the meanings are closely related, but it is often not clear how the two separate readings developed. There is no way of telling simply from the character which reading is intended, and, as so often in Chinese, it is the context that gives the specific meaning.

Yáng

yáng (pronounced *yaang*) meaning yang, sun

The idea of Yin and Yang, complementary and interdependent opposites, is one that the West has embraced eagerly. Yang stands for all things bright, strong, active, and hot. Its elements are Fire and Wood. In Chinese creation mythology, the Heavens were created from the concentration of Yang, and Yang therefore stands for all that is stable and serene. One of the guiding principles of Traditional Chinese Medicine is the idea of keeping up a constant, balanced of flow of Yin and Yang throughout the body to maintain health.

Yì

yì (pronounced *eee*) meaning righteousness

This character represents another of the key virtues of Confucianism, along with filial piety, benevolence, correct conduct, and wisdom. 義 *yì* consists of knowing and acting on what is right. Action should come from a natural knowledge of what is right, not through a deliberate desire to follow a certain course. Confucius said, 'The mind of the superior man turns naturally to righteousness, the mind of the mean man turns to gain.' The first step in cultivating righteousness is recognizing and ridding oneself of prejudice.

Yīn

yīn (pronounced *yin*) meaning yin, shade

Yin and Yang are not two separate concepts but rather they are two points in the continuous ebb and flow of natural rhythm. If the crashing force of an incoming wave is expressive of Yang, the equally powerful outgoing undertow is Yin. Each is preparing for one and neither is possible without the other. Yin is associated with decline and decay, with rivers, valleys, shade, and darkness. Its elements are Water, Metal and Earth, and it is nurturing, yielding, and receptive.

Yīn yuè

yīn yuè (pronounced *yin yweh*) meaning music

Although 樂 *yuè* by itself does actually mean music in classical Chinese, this combination of it preceded by the character for sound 音 *yīn* is the current usage. Music in China hit a low point in the 40 years following the establishment of the People's Republic in 1949, when it was harnessed principally for propaganda purposes. Today, however, as China opens up economically, there have been huge advances in artistic freedom, and Beijing and Shanghai boast some of the most vibrant music and club scenes in the world.

Yīng

yīng (pronounced *ying*) meaning brave, England

英國 *yīng guó* 'brave country' is the Chinese for England. The major foreign powers that China encountered during the Qing Dynasty (1644–1912) – England, France, Germany, and America – were all given names in Chinese that both resembled their sounds in their native languages, and also had auspicious and honorable meanings. Thus, England is brave, France is the country of law, Germany is virtuous, and America beautiful.

Yǒng

yǒng (pronounced *yoong*) meaning eternal

An elegantly simple character, the combination of 水 *shuǐ*, water, and a single dot above it seems to suggest an eternally gushing fountain. This is also a particularly important character in the study of calligraphy, the art of beautiful writing, which is so exquisitely used in Chinese painting. Although it is written using only five strokes, within those five strokes the eight different types of brush movement, from which all characters are composed, are represented.

Yǒng

yǒng (pronounced *yoong*) meaning brave

In this character, it is possible to see a man (男) wearing a helmet, so he must be a soldier, and the qualities of a good soldier are fearlessness and courage. In Chinese thinking, courage is an expression of Qi, energy, and like Qi, must be balanced and controlled by other virtues, or it can be bad as well as good. Confucius said: 'A courageous soldier who lacks righteousness will be disobedient. A courageous civilian who lacks righteousness will become a thief.'

Yōu

yōu (pronounced *yo*) meaning grief, mourning

This character originally symbolized mourning for one's parents, considered the correct conduct of an obedient child. Traditions for mourning were very strict. Funeral rites for an elder had to follow the approved form and be performed fully even if it meant the family went into debt. An unmarried son who died could not be brought home, nor should his parents offer prayers for him. If an infant or child died, no funeral rites were performed because respect was not to be shown to a younger person. A child was buried in silence.

友誼

Yǒu yì

yǒu yì (pronounced *yo see*) meaning friendship

In Confucianism, friendship has a unique but unclear role. It is considered one of the five human relationships that superior men must observe to maintain the fabric of society. The others are between father and son, ruler and subject, husband and wife, and older and younger brother. Confucius himself praises the merits of friendship, but many of his later followers are very wary of it because it lies outside of the settled framework of family and state. Confucius himself wrote: 'Have no friends not equal to yourself.'

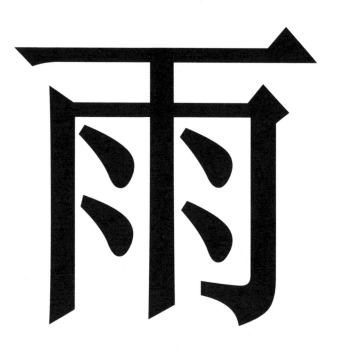

Yǔ

yǔ (pronounced *eeew*) meaning rain

It is easy to see how this character developed from an oracle bone pictogram depicting drops of rain falling from a cloud. As well as meaning rain as a character on its own, it is also the all-purpose 'weather' radical as in, for example, 雷 *léi* thunder. Its appearance in the character 電 *diàn* electricity is only puzzling until you think of lightning. Sadly this connection between ancient and modern, and nature and man's harnessing of it, is no longer there in the simplified version of *diàn*, which simply looks like this: 电.

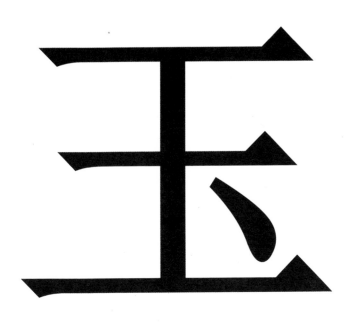

Yù

yù (pronounced *eeew*) meaning jade, precious

Jade has always been considered the most precious material in Chinese culture and has been worked for more than 7,000 years. Confucius said that there are 11 virtues in jade, which can be compared to those in people. In ancient times it was used to protect the body after death. During the Western and Eastern Han Dynasties (206 BCE–220 CE) royalty were buried in suits made entirely of individual jade tiles bound together with gold wire. Nowadays, used in jewels, jade symbolizes long life, beauty, nobility, and power.

Yuè

yuè (pronounced *yweh*) meaning moon, month

This character began life as a pictogram showing a crescent moon and has not changed much over 3,500 years. The moon and its phases have been central to Chinese beliefs and customs from as far back as about 7500 BCE. The traditional Chinese calendar, also known as the Farmers' Calendar is, of course, lunar, meaning that festival dates change each year. After the Spring Festival, or New Year, the next most important date is the Mid-Autumn/Moon Festival, which falls on the fifteenth day of the eighth lunar month.

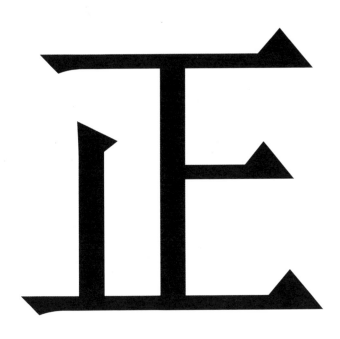

Zhèng

zhèng (pronounced *joong*) meaning upright, correct

Even the appearance of this character seems to illustrate the concept of correctness and decency that it represents.
It covers a huge range of meanings within that broad overall idea: upright, true, orthodox, correct, regular, authorized, exact, straight, formal, just, at the time of, during, to adjust, to regulate, to correct, principal, chief, original, right side, first month of lunar year, middle of a target, whole, entire, without fractions.

Zhì

*zhì (pronounced jrrr) meaning will,
determination, purpose*

This character is made up of a scholar above a heart.
A phrase crucial to the understanding and practice of all the
martial arts, 志師氣 *zhì shī qì* means that Qi is controlled by
the will. Until relatively recently in the People's Republic,
同志 *tóng zhì* translated as comrade, and was the universal
form of address for both men and women. It is seldom heard
outside officialdom these days.

Zhì

zhì (pronounced *jrrr*) meaning knowledge

The Chinese believe that even if someone lives by all the virtues of Confucianism, they still need wisdom to guide them. If a virtuous person is not led by wisdom, his or her virtues are pointless. Confucius said of 智 *zhì*: 'By three methods we may learn wisdom: first, by reflection, which is noblest; second, by imitation, which is easiest; and third by experience, which is the bitterest.'

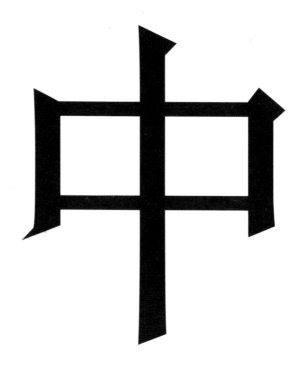

Zhōng

zhōng (pronounced *joong*) meaning middle, China

Originally a pictogram showing an arrow hitting the middle of a target, this character's most important meaning is now integral to the name of China, 中國 *zhōng guó*, the Middle Kingdom or Central Nation. This name first appears in the Classic of History, written in the sixth century BCE. Its use, however, certainly predates this, originating in the way that the heads of state of the Western Zhou Dynasty (1066–771 BCE) believed that they were the divinely appointed rulers of the central civilization of creation.

Zhōng

zhōng (pronounced *joong*) meaning honest, faithful

Composed of the character for 'middle' as phonetic and the character for 'heart' as radical, what else could this mean but inner truthfulness? In combination with 恕 *shù* 'reciprocity', Confucius considers these the key principles of conduct: 忠恕達道不遠 *zhōng shù dá bù yuàn,* 'When a man exercises his true nature according to the principles of reciprocity then he is not far from the true path.' Notice the economy of classical Chinese: six characters translate into 22 words in English.

These pages provide an at-a-glance guide to all of the characters in this book, with their most common meaning in English.

愛
Love

棒
Brilliant

變
Change

冰
Ice

兵
Soldier

禪
Zen

昌
Glorious

成
Become

大
Great

道
The Way

風
Wind

豐
Abundant

鳳
Phoenix

福
Good fortune

父
Father

關係
Connections

光
Light

好
Good

和
Harmony

花
Flower

火
Fire

吉
Auspicious

極
Extreme

家
Home

加油
Come on! Go!

劍
Sword

金
Gold

敬
Respect

酒
Wine

酷
Cool!

樂
Happy/Music

雷
Thunder

冷
Cold

禮
Rites

力
Strength

龍
Dragon

美
America

明
Bright

命
Life

母
Mother

木
Wood

男
Male

女
Female

平安 Peace	氣 Energy	錢 Money	強 Strong	巧 Clever
清 Clear	熱 Hot	仁 Benevolence	日 Sun	石 Stone
壽 Long life	囍 Double happiness	水 Water	死 Death	太 Supreme
土 Earth	武術 Martial arts	舞 Dance	笑 Smile	孝 Filial piety
心 Heart	新 New	信 Belief	性 Sex	幸 Lucky
興 Flourish	陽 Yang	義 Righteousness	陰 Yin	音樂 Music
英 Brave	永 Eternal	勇 Brave	憂 Grief	友誼 Friendship
雨 Rain	玉 Jade	月 Moon	正 Upright	志 Will
智 Knowledge	中 Middle	忠 Honest		

Index

abundant **19**
alcohol, wine **36**
auspicious **29**

beautiful, America **44**
belief, trust **73**
benevolence 58
brave **83**
brave, England **81**
bright **45**
brilliant, great,
  excellent **9**

change **10, 15**
clear, pure **56**
clever, skilled **55**
cold **40**
come on! go! **7, 32**
connections **23**
cool! **37**

dance **7, 68**
Dao **17**
day, sun **59**
death **64**
double happiness **62**
dragon **43**

earth **66**
eternal **82**
extreme, utmost **30**

fate **4**
father **22**
female, woman **50**
filial piety,
  dutifulness **70**
fire **28**
flourish, prosper **76**
flower **5, 27**

friendship **85**

glorious,
  prosperous **14**
glory **24**
go! **7**
gold, metal, money **34**
good **25**
good fortune **21**
great **16**
grief, mourning **84**

happiness, double **62**
happy/music **38**
harmony **26, 51**
heart **71**
home, family **31**
honest, faithful **93**
hot, heat **57**
ice **11**

jade, precious **87**

knowledge **91**

life, fate **4, 46**
light, radiance,
  glory **24**
long life **61**
love **8**
lucky **6, 75**

male **49**
martial arts **67**
metal, gold, money **34**
middle, China **92**
money **34, 53**
moon, month **88**
mother **47**
music **38, 80**

new **72**

peace, harmony **51**
phoenix **20**
prosperous **14**

Qi **52**
radiance **24**
rain **86**
respect **35**
righteousness **78**
rites, correct behaviour **41**

sex **74**
shade **79**
smile, laugh **69**
soldier **12**
stone, rock **60**
strength, power **42**
strong **54**
sun **59, 77**
supreme **65**
sword **33**

thunder **39**

upright, correct **89**

water **63**
will, determination, pur-
pose **90**
wind **18**
wine, alcohol **36**
wood **48**

Yang **77**
Yin **77, 79**

Zen **13**